The Water

Between Us

1998 Agnes Lynch Starrett
Poetry Prize

Pitt Poetry Series

Ed Ochester, Editor

The Water
Between Us

Shara McCallum

University of Pittsburgh Press

For my grandparents,

to Steve,

with love.

Published by the University of Pittsburgh Press, Pittsburgh, Pa. 15261
Copyright © 1999, Shara McCallum
All rights reserved
Manufactured in the United States of America
Printed on acid–free paper
10 9 8 7 6 5 4 3 2

Acknowledgments are located at the end of this book.

Library of Congress Cataloging-in-Publication Data
McCallum, Shara, 1972–
 The water between us / Shara McCallum.
      p.   cm. – (Pitt poetry series)
   ISBN 0-8229-5710-8 (pbk. : alk. paper)
   1. Jamaican Americans Poetry. 2. Mothers and daughters Poetry.
3. Women immigrants–United States–Poetry. I. Title. II. Series.
   PS3563.C33446 W38 1999
   811'.54–dc21   99-6564

Only the magic and the dream are true.
All the rest's a lie.

—Jean Rhys, *Wide Sargasso Sea*

Contents

I

In the Garden of Banana and Coconut Trees

Before the woman's hips
would come to sashay
to other rhythms,
before the man's hands
would grow still, leave
the hollowed-out wood body,
before she would take lovers
over her children,
before his mind would lose
itself to songs
of angels and demons,
before the gospel and herb,

there was my mother,
cooking cornmeal porridge,
plantains, and callaloo for later,
my father's guitar notes,
streaming in from the garden
to hold her singing,
his music, breathing,
lifting leaves
that would collect and stir
at his feet, my mother's
clapping hands, bells jingling
on her ankles.

Apple

Father,
watching you peel the fruit,
knife flat against flesh,
your fingers taut, white at the knuckles,
strips of skin flayed and falling
to the ground,
I think I love you
as Eve must have loved her father
when He turned her out
with the man who only knew
how to follow,
while He sat in the garden
eating the white meat
with the serpent.

Pleasant Hill

This is the house you don't want to remember.
This is the way the hill inclines so steeply
no one can walk up its gravelled path,
no one can hear the child crying in the crib.

Outside, the mother and father watch branches
whispering to leaves. Dishes in the kitchen
sing to pots. In hallways,
rugs cling to sliding floors.

Years later, they will say ghosts dwelled
in the house on Pleasant Hill. The mother will say
remember the black black night:
so still yet filled with crickets

trilling their children to sleep in the tall grass:
green waves moving about her feet.
The father will say remember
the stone-covered drive—

a place no car, trike, nor foot
would tread past midnight
and not dread the feeling of sinking
into the earth, of being lowered

deeper and deeper into a pit
of its own making. This is how
they will each fashion the truth—
piece by piece by piece until

the driveway, the single tree
against a moonless night,
will be all that's left to the memory
of the child waiting to be hushed.

8 Hope Road

This is not my story:
I am walking down my old street

watching trees and flies unmoving,
the man pruning bushes or

drinking whiskey on his verandah,
the woman pinning laundry

on clotheslines, little girls dancing
in the circle of their game.

This is not what I wanted to write,
not what I intended to tell you.

Remember Heidi, instead, coming back
up the mountain, finding Grandfather,

the goats, missing. No note, no
explanation. The gate swinging

on its hinges, milk left to curdle
in the pitcher on the table.

Poem Where My Mother and Father Are Absent

My sisters and I
on the winding path:
the side of the mountain
leading to the river.

One of us getting sick
in the back of Aunty's car;
all of us swaying together
unable to stop.

Our nakedness,
white as sunlight;
a fisherman and his son
watching: our small bottoms

emerging from clear water,
smooth stones underneath;
our submerged bodies
exposed to no one.

Aunty scrubbing
against harder rocks,
trying to get stains out;
her girlfriend fixing lunch.

My sisters and I
running with outstretched arms;
the river calling us
to come back in,

to stay among reeds,
stay floating
in its steady stream,
not return to the house

of broken windows,
thorn-covered walls,
the empty porch swing
creaking in the wind.

What I Saved

for Leah

You
drinking Milo,
then peeling off your nightie, running around the house
with only your panty in place.

That night
you were bitten by scorpion.
The sight of your outstretched leg, shorter than my arm,
puffing up pink and red.

The iron sink
in the backyard
where Clorox clouded the water and your dirty knappies
floated clean.

Your first bath
in a foreign tub.
Your tongue unable to form an *r* as you called
my name.

The Perfect Heart

I am alone in the garden, separated
from my class. This is what comes
of trying to make the perfect heart.

Scissors: silvery cold and slipping
through my four-year-old fingers.
I did not know and took the harder route,

tried to carve a mirrored mountain top
from each center of the page
after page of red construction paper.

Now, I am counting the frangipani
in bloom. Teacher's words still shriller
than the mockingbird's. My cheeks,

wet and hot from more than heat.
If I had been taught, if
once I had been shown the way,

I would have obeyed—not been
a *spoiled, rude, wasteful little girl.*
Folding the paper in two,
I would have cut away the crescent moon.

Fruit

Spaghetti sliding
down our kitchen wall;
pots and pans thrown out,
left to rust in backyard dirt;
my sisters and I crouched
behind the gas stove.

When headmistress beat me
with the cane for being late
again, I didn't cry.
When other children laughed
at my unpolished shoes, unstarched shirt,
I laughed with them.

You were always so proud of me.
What a good girl I was: cleaning,
keeping house, caring for the picknies . . .
You liked showing me off to your men.

What a special mango doll I made:
peeling off skin, revealing the fruit,
saving the dried-out seed
to paint a smiling face upon.

The Feast to Celebrate His Majesty's Birthday

When I woke, I could hear them bleating.
All night rain had come down,
grey and steady, over and around our house.
The soil was soft. I could barely hear footsteps
of the men approaching
but knew they had started
by the sound of splintering
wood, the odour of burning grass.

Squinting against the sun, I watched
a caterpillar crawl up the drying banana leaf.
She looked like one I had caught before,
placed in an empty marmalade jar
and fed till she sprouted wings.
Outside, I heard mummy sweeping,
asking God *how to sing His song*
in this strange land.

When the bleating stopped,
her voice rose above the silence,
ordering me to come help the sistas
clean out the goats, saying no picknie
a ers would gwann like she too good.
Mornings now, I wake in different rooms
to her voice still echoing,
yu hear me? yu hear me gal?

First Rites

At the top of the mountain
I laid on the ground.
Sistas gathered, singing, clapping.

Older girls crouched together,
speaking of blood that stains
baggies, insides of parted thighs

if you are not steeped
deep in the river
and washed clean.

She had taken me from St. Margaret's
wearing my red uniform.
Passing bamboo and sugarcane,

we had walked to reach the river,
to hear the women chanting
whut a ting selassie whut a ting,

to learn what she had always known:
blood does not show itself on red cloth,
hands disappear under running water,

and if you close your eyes quickly,
you will see nothing,
think it is the face of God.

Mother,

what were the angels' demands?
What did you hear from that choir?
One by one, pulled from sleeping hands

then carted across sands
to reach the rising fire.
What were the angels' demands?

The rabbit's glass eyes were the brand,
you said, *of its wicked desire.*
One by one, pulled from sleeping hands

because pig is unclean meat and
the dog has fleas in its fake fur.
What did these angels demand?

In the light, your face turned bland,
your blonde hair sprung like bristling wire
as you pulled each one from sleeping hands,

taking them, you whispered, *to better lands,*
placing them carefully atop the pyre
to satisfy the angels' demands.
One by one, pulled from sleeping hands.

The Awakening

My mother is pinned to the clothesline,
blonde hair billowing like sails in the wind.

The mango dolls return to reclaim their flesh,
whittled off then eaten to secure the seed.

Ants cover the hammock where my father sleeps:
a sea of crimson creeping across white cloth.

They remove the faces we had given them: eyes
that watched, ears that listened, a mouth unable to open.

My sisters and I clear the rotted field,
felling sugarcane with our machetes.

Painted into a frozen smile,
all these years they have lain silent.

jack mandoora me no choose none

we do not really mean,
we do not really mean,
that what we are going to say is true.
—*Ashanti tale*

~~ 1

it begins when the mother
             wants rampion   more than her child:
when this weed grows   in the mind   twists itself   into the heart
        causing vanity   to overpower   love

when the father will   consent   to the old woman   to his wife
        not fight to regain   his daughter   himself
                lost   not heard from again

                                        this is where it begins
                                             always
                                        and where it begins
                                                  again

when the mother
        would rather have straw
spun into gold   unable
        to turn her face   from the golden light
                                        would rather become queen
                                                than know the child she will bear

when the father is not present (as before)   obsequious
        to the woman   conceding to her
                by his absence

17

it is the same story   enchantment
    answers the call of many names:

                        rapunzel   *rumpelstiltskin*
        the old granny   locking the child in the tower
           believing
    this is the way   you save someone
        climbing up hair   beholding the face
                        of betrayal

the little man whose fingers bleed
    from
    spinning
    gold
        who returns
        to the room   thrice
        offering blood
        to receive   life

           other characters not intending harm
           (the messenger discovering the name
                altering destiny
           denying the little man   the child
           he would have loved)

  fury: stamping yourself into the ground   tearing your body into two parts
        this is the true proof
           who loves the child   more

~~ 2

once upon a time in a land of banana and coconut trees
beautiful princesses married whoever could guess their names
bradda anancy was de smartes spider in jamaica: im always foolin
                                                    every oda creature

me remember papa
        use to tell plenty stories   bout anancy
dem always start   wid anancy walkin down de street
        lookin   fi smbady im can fas wid

                                    dat de way
                                    anancy stay
                                                im always wan
                        fi push up imself   inna every oda person business
                        (so we sey fas im fas)

                    anancy de bigges ginel me can tink of
                                    always trickin people an doin mischief

one time   anancy trick bradda gator
                        to tek im cross de river   widout pay im far de trip

anoda time   anancy trick some creature
        fi give up im magic calabash

                        much weepin an wailin
                        an gnashin a teet did gwann
                        afta anancy tief way   dat magic calabash
                            lawd it was someting fi see
                        what oda ting yu tink
                        coulda fill up wid nuf food:

                                        bammy an salfish
                                        ackee an plaintain
                                        rice an peas
                                        breadfuit an yam
               if yu
                  did know   de special words
                                              fi call out
          calabash   *calabash*   *calabash*
               mek it rise up full again

me grandfather use to tell me
          im no know what mek anancy   stay so wutless
               dat it mus be   im jus mek dat way
                              whole eap a time   me hood ask me papa
                         ow anancy   could affec
                                              so many people life
                         an no seem fi care   bout im part in it
me papa sey
               yu caan splain   wha mek some people
                    ac de way dey do
               any more dan yu can sey
                    wha mek tings go
                    de way dey go
                                        im sey yu mus forget
                                        yu mus no wan   fi know so much
                                        yu mus jus haccep
                                        tings appen dat way

                                        jack mandoora me no choose none

20

~~ 3

in some stories   you have no choice
                    you can't remember
                              the truth
          it is not possible
                    to go back
                         to uncover
                                   cause
          discover
                    who really
                         is at fault

so you have to say
                    is anancy do it
          you have to say
                    an evil witch   cast a spell
                                   forget
                                        she was overlooked
                                        not considered to bless
                                                  the child
you have to remember   only
                              the spinning wheel
                              drops of blood
                              light   leading the child   from her parents

     then   it is not
                    the mother
                    the father
                                   it is only a story
          you are trying
                         to remember
                              (to forget)

21

~~ 4

if yu wan fi know why
    mongoose nyam up chicken only
    why im so scarnful a meat
             listen carefully:

one time   farmer give anancy and mongoose   dem pick a two rope
   fi choose   one a im animal dem
               an anancy rope lead im to de fowl

     anancy   being anancy   was vex
       afta im mek   such a poor choice
            an tink up a plan   fi spite mongoose
  (forget   se im spose to be frien to mongoose)

                tiefin de cow
             mongoose chose
         anancy cut off de tail
       id it inna de groun   (wid only one en stickin out)
     an tell mongoose   im cow walk down dere
  never fi come back
            (same time now offerin im chicken
            to mongoose
            fi mek imself look good)

     now mongoose will only eat fowl meat

  no matter   if you were to tell him
             the truth
  take him back   show him   how anancy deceived him
              it wouldn't matter

to this day   mongoose   will not hear you
      he will not forgive
            that cow for deserting him

                    some say
                    it is just a matter of taste
                    that mongoose grew
                    unaccustomed to certain flesh

but i say   is anancy cause it   is anancy mek it   it is anancy
                        who started it

                 jack mandoora me no choose none

~~ 5

in cinderella

       in snow white

          the mother

             who lets vanity

                 overpower her

cannot be   the real mother

          for a real mother   would love her child

                    before herself

the king   cannot be present

          for a father   (present)

     would protect his daughter

               (this is how the stories are told
               this is the way they want you
               to believe them
               this is the account offered up
               as the true tale)

long time ago   when a mother did still love har picknie
    dere was a oman name Ma Kayke
                         an har daughta (Dora)
   when de fada a de gal gone away   de gal mumma fraid
      fi lef har alone   fraid se some man   hooda come
         an wan fi tief   har precious chile away

she lock up de gal inna de house
              an mek up dis song   fi lek har know se
                  is er mumma a knock pan de door
                            when she dah come:

                        Jack-man Dora, fi me Dora
                        Dora Dora bring de lock a paley oh!
                        Dah Ma Kayke dah me ere
                        Dah Ma Kayke dah me ere
                        Dah Ma Kayke—shwee blam!
    dis way   de young gal
   could hopen up de door   widout being scardy-scardy

                me caan remember all de tings dat appen
                or ow anancy get imself mix up inna dis story
       me ongly know se   de daughta   an har mumma
            get separate   by anancy trick

                    long time now
                    me tryin to tell dis story
                    to mek some trut
                    whole eap a time
                    me sidung pan me chair

tryin to repeat

        to remember

               to ear   again

to unforget

      to mek   whole

               parts

                    yu undastan?

smbady mussa cause it   no se is anancy?   im always startin everyting

    a beg to aks yu

        if is not anancy   is who?

              jack mandoora me no choose none

granny tells me the story of hansel and gretel:

    when they lost their way   in the woods

        trees would not help them
               the moon   only a sliver
                     in the night sky
     stars moved
          too quickly   to be guides

                 they had to forget
                 the breadcrumbs
the mother
       abandoning them
         for her hunger

the father   protesting meekly
        turning back   to his block of wood

    granny says the children   should have loved   the witch

              liquorice
              candy canes
              and gingerbread

          were meant for them   all along

    when she asked
       who is nibbling at my house?

they could have answered

it is us granny: your true children come home

then   it would have all been different

if the children
had remembered
the first journey back:
narrow passage through moonlight
only white pebbles to call

                    mother   father

they would have resisted   wanting jewels
                              for those who had forsaken them

        if the witch had been loved   more

                              she would never have put hansel
                              in the cage
                              having his heart
                              why would she hunger
                              for his flesh?
        she would never have made gretel
        prepare the furnace
        gnawing her fingers
        like the chicken bone

she would have loved them   (as she had not loved her own child)

        saving them
                from the axe
                        chopping steadily
                                into the silent woods

II

What Lies Beneath

The woman inside turns flour to dumplings
with the magic of water and salt.
Her hands move without thought.

Outside her window, girls gather,
whispering secrets in corners,
laughing at jokes she can't hear.

She is their age again, home in Trinidad—
swimming out to a nearby dock and falling
asleep in the afternoon sun. Night:

and the shore retreats from her reach;
the water fills with shadows. She hears
her father calling from land's edge.

Why doesn't she answer? Why is she afraid
with his voice instructing her path home?
She has forgotten this story a long time now.

Chopping carrots, her hands become the flashing knife.
Fingers dashing from bag to board, she pauses
to brush a loose hair from her eyes,

trying not to see herself shivering
in the cooling air, the sea beneath her
kept at bay by a few pieces of wood.

Debt

for my grandmother

All day she scrubs the house:
each tile, strip of wall, thorn
of each rose in the vase.

All day she polishes the desk,
readying it for work, polishes
the work off quickly,

making checks on her list.
What has she forgotten?
How many times can she

wash her hands?
How much is obsession
weighed against need?

How many nights
enough to pay?
How many minutes

past two before sleep
becomes permissible?
This poem.

This too is not enough.

The Spell

A hag is riding my back.
Darkness steals into my pores.
One cold hand encircles my throat;
the other coils around my hair, reining me
close enough to taste her soured breath.
I settle the broom beneath the bed,
sprinkle water on all four corners of the spread,
but her eyes burn into my dreams.
All night, she feasts on my flesh
and the wind breaks through the eaves.
In sleep, I twist to glimpse her face.
But the moon turns to stone.

The Evolution of Useful Things

Consider a hammer
striking a nail:
bludgeoning this object resisting
where it's being told to go.

Consider this same hammer
building a house:
binding disparate wood,
knowing paint will yield
a sheen of similarity.

Consider this hammer, thinking,
I'm just doing my job.

See the house
standing through snow:
girding itself against
that scrap of sky it blocks and opposes.

See the house
weathering: paint
chipping in places,
shingles loose,
shutters disheveled—
hanging at odd angles
like broken limbs.

poppies

in the corner of a room
a picture will fall suddenly
and a hand will appear to right it

later this will happen again

(silently)

like poppies growing
in a field
    full
in their redness
but expecting
       snow

What the Stories Teach

The man playing the flute
always gets what he wants:
unsuspecting babes
forsake trikes, toss dolls
face down in the dirt, leave
mommy and daddy's good night
kiss and tuck to dust.
Skipping and singing into the silent sea,
the last head descends into the water
the way an apple vanishes
beneath the caramel glaze.

Dove

Imagine if you could have either *cherry* or *stove*,
but not both; if the sound of rain
would not answer to its name: *tap, tap, pitter pat.*
If one morning you woke and had to say *dove*,
not *love*, and mean it. If this went on
all through the day and night and into early dawn—
this calling of the world and all its parts
a single word: your cat's meow,
the kumquat freshly washed at the sink,
the milk bottle in the fridge, swallows
outside listing on the wind, the grey slant
of falling rain, a lover's hand grazing your neck.

For you sweetheart,

I'll forget I have a name.
You can call me *honey, sweet Jesus, my God*.
I'll answer,
yes baby, ooh sugar, um-hmm.
I'll watch you grind
cigarette butts into the ashtray
all afternoon long, forget
about clothes needing to come in off the line,
that roast needing basting in the oven,
unattended weeds growing wild in the yard.
I'll bring you gin after gin
to watch your tongue
slide up and down the side
of the sweating glass.
For you sweetheart,
I'll tell my family Sundays
are an awful day to visit, apologise
when I see Reverend Maxwell
at the market, find an excuse
to wear nothing around the house,
complaining of constant heat.
I'll lean across your body,
fluff pillows
for the hundredth time,
just to smell aftershave
mixed with sweat. I'll bend over,
pick up your paper
to feel your gaze move
up and down my back.
For you sweetheart,

I'll water the hibiscus
four times a day,
press my lips together,
praying to buds
sheathed in green,
knowing you love
to watch flowers bloom.

Something Like Flying

for Steven

You point them out to me:
the geese flying straight over us,
emerging from the trees as though
they have been on the other side
the whole time, waiting for us
to reach this stretch of woods.

In an instant their bodies
seem near enough to touch.
Exchanging places in the line,
weaving a jagged, v-shaped
ribbon of grey, they diminish
in size over your shoulder.

You tell me they fly
in this pattern all the way
of their long journey
over housetops and trees,
passing schoolyards and churches,
leaving everything

they've known, as I stand here,
studying your face, following
their flight to Brazil, Jamaica,
or some other shore: one of them
growing tired and falling behind,
another coming up to take the lead.

The Remains

I left the knife in the sink,
rind coiled around it,
sharp scent of citrus
unfurling in the air.

I left the magazine open
to the picture of a woman,
a man in the shadow,
her face in terror.

The garbage by the door,
I left undone with care:
last night's fish strewn
over last week's stew.

All for you to find,
dearest. All I left for you to find.

Darkling I Listen

If I could write the truth,
I would remove all words
that are beautiful, like *dying*
and *disease* and *pain*.

I would use a paring knife
to gut the flesh of your cheeks,
polish bones underneath
till they gleamed white.

I would slice open your arms,
pull out veins that won't give up
their blood to any more needles,
pull hard enough to release words

inside your body: the dream you told me
about the landscape eating itself
and moulting; the silence
of cannibal grass and trees.

III

May 1981

I was leaving my ninth year
when the rain began;
when the cicada forgot her song;
the tree frog's throat shut down;
crickets left the tall grass of the valley
for the mountain's higher ground;
when peacocks would not bloom;
goats refused the hills, started a path
to the sea; chicks would not take
corn from my outstretched palm.
When my father and the man
with hair of coiling flames
each turned away his face.

What I'm Telling You

My father played music. He played a guitar and sang. My father recorded his songs in the same studio where Bob Marley played with his band. And if you know who Bob is and are thinking "One Love," dreadlocks, ganja, *hey mon,* then you are straying from the center of this poem, which is the recording studio where I slept on the floor while my father sang and strummed his guitar. And where Bob, who was only a brother in Twelve Tribes to me at four or five, said to the man who called me *whitey gal* that I was not, that I was a daughter of Israel, that I was Stair's child. That same Bob who you've seen shaking his natty dreads and jumping up and down; that same man with the voice of liquid black gold became a legend in my mind too at four or five as a record somewhere in a studio in Jamaica started to spin.

Sunset on the Wharf

John crows fill the red sky. Coming in
closer with each swooping pass, they smell

the unsold dead to be discarded. Fishermen,
women with their wares, higglers, pack up

as daylight ends. My father's presence lingers.
With an eight-year-old's eyes, I watch him poised

on one leg, frozen in the midst of motion. Right
leg straight, firmly planted in the soil. Left one

bent at the knee, stranded in midair. Walking:
the unfinished step he could not make.

My calling could not retrieve him from that place
he exchanged for me: no *Daddy, Father, Alastair,*

enough to reclaim the eyes averted from my gaze.
What he saw, what he went toward, I was left

behind, pulling at his sleeve as people crowded to see
the spectacle: my father: standing grasshopper,

lotus flower against darkening seas, sand turning black,
grains disintegrating under the dying light of the sun.

Losing Footing

Did your father's breathing become the rasping
night? When you walked in the garden,

did you call to the mockingbird and hear locusts
answer back? Did your mother make you sit

with hands folded in the corner? Did she
go on counting the pieces of her puzzle,

forbidding you to touch even one?
Did starch give your shirts life,

binding your arms with sleeves
that wrapped around your form

like a body pressing against your own?
When you saw the sun each dawn, did you forget

what colour it would appear or not know where
it would go next? When you found the gully

for the first time, did you lose your sense of depth—
not realise the earth could stoop so low, so quickly?

When you played in the leaves, gathering
in the slow-moving stream,

what made you see tears and blood beneath skin
as you lifted your palms to the light?

What We Forget

He died the same month
flamingo-coloured Miami
became the realised promised land
of air conditioning, television
and McDonald's. He died
the same day she was playing hopscotch:
newly sketched chalk boxes
on the walk outside her grandparent's home.
And she remembers long before,
clasping a yellow flower around the bee
that tried to escape her desire
to hold beauty in her palm.
And she remembers him
sucking the stinger from her thumb
but cannot recall the touch
of his lips pressed tight to her flesh,
the tingling of her skin being healed.

Jamaica, 1978

It was always about the coconut tree:
in the back a the house, beside the iron sink;
so close, a coconut would often fall down
badam pon our wet clothes. Under there
we would tek our dollies for tea parties,
meking mud pies outta its earth;
under that same tree, mummy did fling out
we pots an pans one day when she get vex;
is there we would run when beatings was to come.
When we was getting too big an boasy,
mummy would warn, *Chicken merry. Hawk near.*
But we'd go on bad, same way, as all picknie likely fi do.

Me no know why we would choose that tree.
There was plenty other one in the yard.
Mango is good for climbing: we coulda scale it fast
if we knew she was behin an not likely fi follow.
Banana have much fatter leaf an trunk
an was farther away from the kitchen stoop:
she woulda haffa come roun the side a the house
an search good. But no, it was always coconut
we go look protection—even when the trunk so skinny
it couldn't afford four a we no hiding place
from what was in store; the branch them so flimsy flimsy,
yu haffa aks yuself: is who this tree go a shade from sun?

Jamaica, October 18, 1972

You tell me about the rickety truck:
your ride in back among goats or cows—
some animal I can't name now—

the water coming down your legs,
my father beside you, strumming
a slow melody of darkened skies

and winter trees he only dreamed
on his guitar. The night was cool.
That detail you rely on each time

the story is told: the one story
your memory serves us better
than my own. I doubt even that night

you considered me, as I lay inside you,
preparing to be born. So many nights
after it would be the same.

You do not remember anything,
you say, so clearly as that trip:
animal smells, guitar straining for sound,

the water between us becoming a river.

Persephone Sets the Record Straight

You are all the rage these days,
mother. Everywhere I turn, I hear
Demeter in mourning, Demeter
grieving . . . poor Demeter.

Always craving the spotlight,
I know this is what you wanted:
your face on the front page
of all the papers; gossip columns

filled with juicy tidbits
on *what life was like before winter,*
old hags in the grocery store, whispering,
how she's let the flowers go,

while young women hover
in their gardens, fearing their hibiscus
will be next on your hit list.
After all these summers,

you still won't come clean.
Passing me iced tea, instead
you ask, *How's the redecorating?*
Are you expanding

to make room for little ones?
Fanning away flies,
you avoid my eyes, saying,
I've so longed to be a grandma,

you know.
For God's sake, mother,
can't you tell me the truth now it's done?
Just once, tell me

how you put me in that field
knowing he'd come,
that you made snow fall
everywhere to cover your tracks,

that the leaves die still
because you can't punish him
for confirming your suspicions:
not wanting you,

he took me instead.
Of course I ate those seeds.
Who wouldn't exchange
one hell for another?

Mother Love

I know what she knew
and when she knew it.
Standing behind her
in front of the stove.
My words still swirling
in the space between us.
The hem of my dress torn
below one knee. My hands
clutching and unclutching cloth
inside my pockets. The room
spinning darker and darker
like those nights she would leave
and the shadow would descend—
his greedy tongue lapping
up the air around my body.
But she kept sweeping the floor,
stoking the fire. Looked at me
only long enough to say:
Yu dutty little liar.

It's always the same. The white house. A little girl who cannot run, cannot scream, can only take apples for kisses, gum for occupying her tongue. It's always the same man, whiteyellowredbrown, his hands larger than her mouth, crackedorsmooth, roughorsoft against her lips. His lap is a hole. If she moves too close, she will sink. She is never alone. Across the room, her sisters sleeporareawake. Down the hall, she can still see them when it grows against her handsfacebetweenherlegs. The mother is never home. Always that same moonorsun staring on. The windows parted. The door ajar. Bathroombedroomkitchen. Always, the same. When she wakes, the moon still in its place. The water on the table.

What my mother taught me:

When God closes a door, there are no windows.
When the Big Bad Wolf knocks, he knows how to get in.
Be afraid of the dark.

Don't scream.
Don't run.
Don't make wishes you can't keep.

If you drag a horse to water enough, she will drink.
If you don't play with fire, it will find you and burn.
Even careful chickens get caught by the hawk.

Lullaby

Your hands resting
against my scalp;
your fingers and comb—
in unison parting my hair.
The smell of oil; our breathing.
Your low humming
here and there breaking
into words in that voice
only birds understood.
The scent of yellow lye;
your arms like the skin
of a mango, lifting me—
little—into the sink;
your fingers sudsing
the warm cloth.
Your half-lit face
beside mine
in the almost dark,
lowering me into sleep;
your eyelids fluttering
to close down my own.
Only years later
will I wake and search for you,
not know which is the dream.
Empty rooms
swimming in moonlight;
wind blowing in
colder than your kiss.

Discubriendo una Fotografía de Mi Madre

If I had left Venezuela with you, been on the boat moving
from your world of Papá, Mamá, abuelos, tios, y primos,

I could watch granny cooking en la cocina,
taste frijoles negros y arepas hot on my tongue.

If I had worn your clothes, dressed like this niña bonita
you left behind, I would be able to conjure up the collar

moored to your neck, feel its lace scratching my skin.
If I had the memory you lost to the Atlantic

(the blur of a white house in the background, las caobas
lining the front walk, the music box dancer still spinning

in your hand), if I could do more than imagine you
as this child, I would understand how *tierra, pais,*

y casa became untranslatable words. From Spanish
to Patwa, something nameless must have gone wrong.

Yu no send. Me no come.

The first night back and rain falls,
tinging on the aluminum roof.
Trees my tongue had forgotten
return one by one:
     breadfruit, soursop, ackee.

Bougainvillea weigh
with water, fuchsia petals drip
    in disarray.
Love, when you see me next,
    tell me I've changed.

                          ~~

If we name in order to know:

    say *apple*
        it will taste red.

    say *bird*
        it will fly
        from your mouth.

    say *home*
        see what stays.

In Negril, a bartender asks where I'm from.
    For the hundredth time today I answer:
        Kingston originally.

For the hundredth time I hear:
    Fi true? But yu so light.
        Yu nuh talk Jamaican.

My sister laughs, offering warning:
    Yu betta not call har no yankee gal, papa.
        She will get well vex wid yu.

Living here again,
    she has the right to say:
        Is fi she country too.

~~~

        Long time ago I learned how to mek de ketch arredi grow:
        de key is to bruk off a piece fram de parent
        an plant it inna de groun.

            It will sprout up quick.
            De flower dem will come fas
            and grow same way
            as de original tree.

                Dats why it call *ketch arredi.*
                Dats why it call *never die.*

~~

From my sister's porch, the airport stretches below me.
Beside it, sea comes in to land,
touching borders of vegetation and sand.

I search for the lizard on the nearby branch,
nearly call Renée to show her it is both there
and not there: so green, you might almost miss it.

All around me, hibiscus and banana trees
fringe the planes taking off. I wonder when they leave,
what assures them they will come down?

In my other life,

I was born with a stone in my hand.
My first word was not *muma.*
I learned from early on that *duppy know who to frighten*
and chose carefully.
I learned to *tell the truth an shame the devil,*
to be seen when not heard,
to spell names of places I would someday know
more than my home:
knife an a fork an a bottle an a cork
dats de way yu spell New York;
chicken in de caar an de caar caan go,
dats de way yu spell Chicago.
I took cod liver oil with orange juice each morn.
I ate green mangoes and drank peppermint tea for the bellyache.
I stole otahite apples from the market.
My hands would not listen and often took licks.
I showed the boys my panty because they said I wouldn't.
I ate stinkintoe on a dare.
I knelt down in the dirt and made mud pies.
I climbed tamarind trees, banyan trees, even palms.
I walked barefoot and was not afraid to *ketch cold.*
I tried to catch hummingbirds.
I made bracelets, earrings, and rings from flowers.
I was a queen.
I was a mongoose stealing chicks.
I was a goat on a hillside,
sure of the path.

Seed

I am a child of the sun, balancing
the wind on my hips.
I have learned to make stones
dance, to walk with each footfall
echoing silence, to listen to the songs
of leaves. I am a child of the hushing sea:
waves, the sound of my listening;
salt, the scent of my sight.
I have taken machete to the coconut,
ground sugarcane between my teeth,
to unclasp their sweetened rhymes.
At dawn, I have held the waking earth,
each grain of dirt and sand
spilling from my half-open hands.
Wherever I am, I am
that space between
the husk and the heart
of the fruit.

IV

the sirens' defense

when we sing
they hear their lives retold
in our song
they see the course
they chose not to chart

it is not our voices
drifting across this ocean
steering them
into these rocks

A Warning

I am the shoal you cannot cross;
the barnacles that cling
to the side of your boat.
I am the night sky,
shrouding the stars
you use as a guide;
the crash of the wave
on the planks of your ship.
Tambourines quivering,
far-off flute whistling:
I am that familiar song
to which your mother warned you
not to listen.

Siren Isles

Stranger,
this is not your home.
Fruit blossoming;
coral ringed round my wrist;
honeysuckle days;
jasmine nights;
sea caressing sand:
none of this
is what it appears.
Beneath the surface
of the clear water—
look deep.
I am a fish no desire
will allow you to reach.

I Promise You This

Water finds its own level
means your children will know my name.
In the night, when they dream,
fists curled into their face,
the last sound they hear
will be the ocean filling their ears.
Water finds its own level
means you sank low
and quickly into your grave
when you pulled my body ashore,
tore me from my home and left me
calling for air on that scorched beach.
The freak, the half-woman, half-fish
circus attraction, you shrieked.
And not even eternity could stop
the echo of your howling.
Nor can eternity now diminish
my search: your kin, your kin's kin
for every generation to come,
will fear the rush of the tide,
the swell of the wave,
the hint of water
already filling their cribs.

Enough

Every morning he brings coconut water
still in the husk. He thinks
this will bear my loss.
Afternoons, hired women
adorn my hair with tortoise-shell
combs, mother-of-pearl pins.
He thinks this will make me forget.
But I am no woman
to be bought by small gifts.
All night when he sleeps
I lick the casing of trees,
wandering the garden,
pressing my toes into earth underneath.
Dawn, he finds me once more
like that first day: washed ashore,
unable to move, watching
my body split in two.
He calls me back
in the same way: with sugar
in his voice and palm:
sweet baby please
he coos, offering me the seeds
of his fettered fruit.

The Sea Returns

Mother, mother, I hear the sound at the door,
the roar even closer, the coast
most surely under by now.

Daughta, is the last time I goin aks if yu fine mi cap:
the one yu fada hide from me all these years. Unda bed, unda chair . . .
I just doh know where.

Mother, mother, I see the tip of the crest.
Blue, blue, everywhere, thicker
than the dark of my closed fist.

Daughta, stop yu foolishness now.
Cho. Is dead yu fada gone dead and him nuh even have the grace
fi lek me know where him lef mi blessed cap.

Mother, mother, the waves are closing in.
Water rising up to my chin, over my head . . .
I am lost.

Lookhere, daughta, is home this is, coming back
fi me at last. Cap or no cap, I goin back inna mi skin.
Daughta? Daughta? Daughta? Oh gawd. She caan swim.

The Daughter, Left

In dreams my mother returns:
unmasked and shimmering
below the surface of her skin;
in dreams, I see her hands,
unwrinkled again, gliding
a comb through unmatted hair.
Floating beyond my reach,
far away, as if under water,
she calls: *My daughter,*
you must leave this place,
go down to the sea
and fish for your true face.

When I think of you,

you are still diving into the sea,
swimming away from the reef,
your orange scales flickering
iridescent in the sinking sun.
I call to you once, twice,
then once again. But you leave me
a stream of darkness in your wake.

Calypso

Dese days, I doh even bada combing out mi locks.
Is dread I gone dread now.
Mi nuh stay like dem oda ones, mi luv—
wid mirra an comb,
sunnin demself pon every rock,
lookin man up and down de North Coast.
Tourist season, dem cotch up demself whole time in Negril,
waitin for some fool-fool American,
wid belly white like fish,
fi get lickle rum inna him system an jump in.
An lawd yu should see de grin.
But man can stupid bad, nuh?
I done learn mi lesson long ago
when I was young and craven.
Keep one Greek boy call Odysseus
inna mi cave. Seven years
him croonin in mi ear an him wife nuh see him face.
The two a we was a sight fi envy. I thought
I was goin die in Constant Spring at last
till the day him come to me—
as all men finally do—seyin him tired a play.
Start talkin picknie an home an wife
who can cook an clean. *Hmph.*
Well yu done know how I stay arredi, mi love.
I did pack up him bag and sen him back
to dat oda woman same time.
I hear from Mildred down de way
dat de gal did tek him back, too;
him tell her is farce I did farce him fi stay
an she believe the fool. But lawd,

woman can also bline when she please.
Mi fren, I tell yu,
I is too ole for all dis bangarang.
I hear ova Trini way, young man is beatin steel drum,
meking sweet rhyme an callin music by mi name.
Well, dat the only romance I goin give de time a day.
Hmph.

Apsara

To carry the dead
means we cannot ever live.
What would it be
to own a soul
that yearns for light,
that ascends up through the waves
into the blue
greater than our comprehension?
Who chooses beauty
chooses a fate worse than death.
Do not envy our lot, gentle sailor.
When we cease to breathe,
we will be only that foam breaking
each time you traverse the sea.

Two Sides

〜〜 1. The Apsara Addresses the Fisherman

There is no boat
to hold you up.
Only the sky
immense as the sea,
your body silhouetted by light
rendering your face invisible.
And this net you cast
deeper and deeper into the water,
each time sure
this catch will be the one
to harvest your soul.

〜〜 2. The Fisherman Responds

You are the silver light
darting beneath the surface
of my dream. All night,
I am the fish
fluttering inside your mouth.
I am the water
filling your gills.

The Fisherman's Wife

Each day I will make you
a meal of fish heads soaked
in scallions, scotch bonnets, vinegar,
and wine; cassava pounded flat
beneath my fists, then fried crisp;
roasted plantains; soursop juice
teased with lime. At dusk
before your return, I will
bathe in rose water, oil my scalp,
polish my skin till it glistens
in the coming moonlight
like mother-of-pearl washed ashore.

In time, you will forget
the painted dusk calling you back;
the surf rupturing herself again and again
for the sand's fleeting touch;
the flamboyant sun rising
from beneath the ocean's shell:
her heat swirling across your face
like Salome's last veil come undone.

The Meeting

∿ 1

In school, I kept my papers neat.
My shoes, polished. My pants, creased
in the proper way. My tie, in place.
Mother warned me never to dawdle,
always to come straight home.
I took the right path, time and time again,
when others hopped barbed wire
and scaled walls, risking tears and scrapes.
*Long cut draw sweat but short cut
draw blood*, I would hear mother's heeding
voice repeating in my head.
So why did the sun reflect something different
in the water that day? Why did my eyes stray
from the road ahead, my house
just then visible on the horizon?
Why did I turn and look?

∿ 2

My sisters' first sounds were song.
My own words stayed garbled in my throat.
But that day when he came whistling
down the path nearest the shore,
I heard something ancient
in his forgotten tune, saw some hint
of long ago in the angling of his head
toward the sun. Mother always said:
You can bring a grown man to his knees

with only a look, child. When the time comes
you'll know what to do. Just shake your tail
and be beautiful.
And I did.
God help me, I did.

The Exchange

The first sound was his guitar:
more than the song of the blue whale,
the stirrings in my dreams.
The first sight was his head
bobbing upon invisible waves,
buoying his music along.
And I knew then: it would be better
to drown in this terrible air
than live in the vast, unbridled sea.

The Choice Made

At night I feel the ocean
inspecting my life.
Look what you have become,
the mist shrieks: *Salt*
carving crevices into your cheeks.
You, who were once a queen.

In chorus, waves hurl their curved bodies
again and again against the cliffs;
the tide shakes its foaming head
in disbelief; and the wagging fingers
of the receding surf sprawl my mother's
warning across the sand:

You leave your kind.
Nothing but bad luck will follow
all the days of your life.

The tragedy of the mermaid

is not that she must leave her home
but that she must cast off her flesh.
To love, she must lose scales as a child
relinquishes dolls to youth;
she must hide the shells
she plants under her tongue,
culling her dreams;
she must stop the tide rising
in her breath each night;
she must stem the scent of salt
seeping from her skin.
Touching her shrivelled face,
she must not feel an ocean
falling from her eyes.

What the Oracle Said

You will leave your home:
nothing will hold you.
You will wear dresses of gold; skins
of silver, copper, and bronze.
The sky above you will shift in meaning
each time you think you understand.
You will spend a lifetime chipping away layers
of flesh. The shadow of your scales
will always remain. You will be marked
by sulphur and salt.
You will bathe endlessly in clear streams and fail
to rid yourself of that scent.
Your feet will never be your own.
Stone will be your path.
Storms will follow in your wake,
destroying all those who take you in.
You will desert your children
kill your lovers and devour their flesh.
You will love no one
but the wind and ache of your bones.
Neither will love you in return.
With age, your hair will grow matted and dull,
your skin will gape and hang in long folds,
your eyes will cease to shine.
But nothing will be enough.
The sea will never take you back.

Acknowledgments

Grateful acknowledgment is made to the following publications
in which some of the poems in this collection first appeared,
sometimes in different versions: *Another Chicago Magazine*
("Darkling I Listen"); *Antioch Review* ("Jamaica, October 18, 1972");
Caribbean Writer ("Calypso," "The tragedy of the mermaid," "What
Lies Beneath"); *Chelsea* ("Sunset on the Wharf," "What my mother
taught me:," "Yu no send. Me no come."); *Crab Orchard Review*
("The Feast to Celebrate His Majesty's Birthday," "First Rites," "The
Fisherman's Wife"); *Double Entendre* ("Fruit"); *5AM* ("The Sea
Returns," "What the Oracle Said," "What We Forget"*); Hubbub*
("jack mandoora me no choose none"); *The Iowa Review* ("Apple,"
"In the Garden of Banana and Coconut Trees," "Persephone
Sets the Record Straight"); *Kestrel* ("Apsara," "The Daughter,
Left," "When I think of you"); *Obsidian II: Black Literature in Review*
("The Perfect Heart"); *Quarterly West* ("The Awakening"); *Seneca
Review* ("The Evolution of Useful Things," "poppies"); *Verse*
("Discubriendo una Fotografía de Mi Madre," "Jamaica, 1978");
and *Virginia Quarterly Review* ("In my other life,").

"The Fisherman's Wife" was reprinted in and "What The
Stories Teach" appeared in *The Beach Book: A Literary Companion,*
published by Sarabande Books. "Yu no send. Me no come.,"
"What my mother taught me:," and "Jamaica, October 18, 1972"
will appear in *Beyond the Frontier: An Anthology of Contemporary
African American Poets,* to be published by Black Classic Press.
"Persephone Sets the Record Straight" first appeared in *The Year's
Best Fantasy and Horror,* published by St. Martin's Press.

I wish to extend a very warm thank you to Mr. Carl Abrahams,
one of the foremost Jamaican artists and considered to be "the
father of Jamaican Art" for his permission to use a detail from

his painting *Chopin's Polonaise,* on the cover of the book. My love and deep gratitude to Steven for his patience and support during the composition of these poems and to my family for their enduring faith in me: my grandparents, Sally and David DePass, my mother, Migdalia Bertorelli, my aunts, Yvonne Bertorelli and Susan Ebel, and my sisters, Reneé, Natalia, Shayla, Leah, Karima, and Alanna. To Rose, Al, Joe, Susan, and David, my love and thanks for your support. I am deeply grateful as well to all the friends who have believed in me and sustained me over the years. *Mil gracias a* Denise Cabrera; *muchos abrazos a* Mia Leonin, who has been with this book from the start; many thanks to Melody Elliott and Joelle Biele for their letters and deep friendship; thank you to Paul and Beth Burch, Ivy Kaufman, Emily Orlando, and Michael Pino for being in my corner. To Elizabeth Alexander, Toi Derricotte, Cornelius Eady, Afaa Weaver, and everyone at Cave Canem who provided me a community in which to work, *ashe.* For their insights into the poems, thank you to Kwame Dawes and Sarah Gorham. Thank you to the Graduate School at the University of Maryland and the Clark Foundation at Binghamton University for fellowships which afforded me the time and space to complete these poems. To all of my teachers, my gratitude for the guidance, encourage-ment, and support that have helped to bring me here: Michael Collier, Merle Collins, Nicole King, Joyce Kornblatt, Phillis Levin, Laura Mullen, Stanley Plumly, Liz Rosenberg, Ruth Stone, Susan Strehle, Libby Tucker, Elaine Upton, Mary Helen Washington, and Michael Waters. And to Judith Vollmer for first noticing these poems and Ed Ochester for his keen editorial advice, I am deeply indebted.